GALE
CENGAGE Learning

Novels for Students
Volume 8

Staff

Series Editor: Deborah A. Stanley.

Contributing Editors: Peg Bessette, Sara L. Constantakis, Catherine L. Goldstein, Dwayne D. Hayes, Motoko Fujishiro Huthwaite, Arlene M. Johnson, Angela Yvonne Jones, James E. Person, Jr., Polly Rapp, Erin White.

Editorial Technical Specialist: Tim White.

Managing Editor: Joyce Nakamura.

Research: Victoria B. Cariappa, *Research Team Manager*. Andy Malonis, *Research Specialist*. Tamara C. Nott, Tracie A. Richardson, and Cheryl L. Warnock, *Research Associates*. Jeffrey Daniels, *Research Assistant*.

Permissions: Susan M. Trosky, *Permissions Manager*. Maria L. Franklin, *Permissions Specialist*. Sarah Tomacek, *Permissions Associate.*

Production: Mary Beth Trimper, *Production Director*. Evi Seoud, *Assistant Production Manager*. Cindy Range, *Production Assistant*.

Graphic Services: Randy Bassett, *Image Database Supervisor*. Robert Duncan and Michael Logusz, *Imaging Specialists*. Pamela A. Reed, *Photography Coordinator*. Gary Leach, *Macintosh Artist*.

Product Design: Cynthia Baldwin, *Product Design Manager*. Cover Design: Michelle DiMercurio, *Art Director*. Page Design: Pamela A. E. Galbreath, *Senior Art Director*.

Copyright Notice

Since this page cannot legibly accommodate all copyright notices, the acknowledgments constitute an extension of the copyright notice.

While every effort has been made to secure permission to reprint material and to ensure the reliability of the information presented in this publication, Gale Research neither guarantees the accuracy of the data contained herein nor assumes any responsibility for errors, omissions, or discrepancies. Gale accepts no payment for listing; and inclusion in the publication of any organization, agency, institution, publication, service, or individual does not imply endorsement of the editors or publisher. Errors brought to the attention of the publisher and verified to the satisfaction of the publisher will be corrected in future editions.

This publication is a creative work fully protected by all applicable copyright laws, as well as by misappropriation, trade secret, unfair competition, and other applicable laws. The authors and editors of this work have added value to the underlying factual material herein through one or more of the following: unique and original selection, coordination, expression, arrangement, and classification of the information. All rights to this publication will be vigorously defended.

Copyright © 2000
The Gale Group
27500 Drake Rd.
Farmington Hills, MI 48331-3535

All rights reserved including the right of reproduction in whole or in part in any form.

ISBN 0-7876-3827-7
ISSN 1094-3552

Printed in the United States of America.
10 9 8 7 6 5 4 3 2 1

Kindred

Octavia E. Butler

1979

Introduction

Prior to the publication of her fourth novel, *Kindred*, Octavia Butler was primarily known only to fans of science fiction. While her first three novels—all part of the "Patternmaster" series— received favorable reviews, her work was marginalized as genre fiction. Since the 1979 publication of *Kindred*, however, Butler's work is known to a wider audience.

The novel focuses on many of the issues found in Butler's fiction: the abuse of power, the limits of traditional gender roles, and the repercussions of racial conflict. The science-fiction elements of the story are limited, however, to the unexplained mechanism that permits a twentieth-century Africa American woman to travel into the past. Each time Dana Franklin is drawn back into the early 1800s to save the life of her white ancestor, she learns more about the complex nature of slavery and the struggles of African Americans to survive it. The result is a powerful and accessible story that resembles a historical slave narrative—but one told from a modern perspective and in a modern voice.

Butler's exploration of this era has led many new readers to discover her work, from feminist critics to students of African American literature. These individuals have learned what fans of science fiction have long known: Butler crafts some of the most imaginative and thought-provoking fiction today. "In *Kindred*," Robert Crossley wrote in his introduction to the novel, "Octavia Butler has designed her own underground railroad between past and present whose terminus is the reawakened imagination of the reader."

Butler was born in Pasadena, California, in 1947, and grew up in a racially mixed neighborhood. An only child, she was very young when her father died, and her mother worked as a maid to support the two of them. She was raised as a strict Baptist, a faith that forbade dancing or makeup. For solace and escape, she turned to reading. She became a fan of science fiction magazines; inspired by the possibilities of the genre, she was only twelve when she began writing the first version of what would eventually become her "Patternmaster" novels.

Butler received an associate's degree from Pasadena City College in 1968 and entered California State University in Los Angeles the following year. She left school, however, after discovering there was no creative writing major. She attended several workshops in the late 1960s, including the Writers Guild of America. There she met noted science-fiction writer Harlan Ellison, who became Butler's mentor and helped her gain admittance to the Clarion Science Fiction Writers Workshop in 1970. The six-week course introduced her to several well-known writers.

She supported herself with the kinds of menial jobs that Dana Franklin describes in *Kindred*. In 1976 she published her first novel, *Patternmaster*, the first in a series of works describing a society whose members have developed telepathic powers over the course of centuries. Butler went on to publish five novels in this series.

While in the midst of exploring the "Patternmaster" universe, Butler began to write a novel examining the pain and fear African Americans had to live through in order to endure and succeed in American society. The resulting novel was *Kindred* (1979), a unique exploration of slavery as experienced through a modern woman's eyes.

Butler has been awarded several of science fiction's highest awards for her short fiction, including the Hugo and Nebula Awards. She continues to write science fiction, including the three-volume "Xenogenesis" series and two volumes in her "Earthseed" series. Her protagonists are usually women coming from a black or biracial background, which provides a different perspective to a field dominated by white males for many years.

The River

On her twenty-sixth birthday, Dana, the protagonist of *Kindred*, is overcome by nausea and finds herself on the bank of a river. When she sees a young boy drowning in the river, she jumps in and saves him. She is shocked when the boy's father points a gun at her head; it is clear that he is suspicious of Dana, a young black woman. Suddenly, she finds herself back in her living room. Although she was by the river for minutes, she has been away from home for only a few seconds.

Traumatized by the event, she calms down and begins to recover her wits. Suddenly she finds herself next to the same boy, named Rufus, in a burning bedroom. As she saves him again, Dana realizes that Rufus is calling her when his life is in danger. She discovers that the year is 1815, and although he is a white, Southern slave-owner, he is the future father of the first woman listed in her family records—Hagar Weylin. The woman listed as Ha-gar's mother, Alice Greenwood, is a free black child and Rufus' friend. Dana realizes that she has just saved the life of her ancestor.

Dana decides to visit Alice, but ends up watching as patrollers drag Alice's father out and whip him. He is a slave, and has come to visit his family without permission. A patroller grabs Dana and tries to rape her. She hits him and returns to her life in 1976. When she shares her experiences with her husband, Kevin, he has a hard time believing her. He realizes that Dana can only come back to the present when her life is in danger.

The Fall

The next time that she begins to disappear, Kevin is pulled back in time too. They arrive in a clearing next to Rufus, now twelve years of age, who has a broken leg. Rufus' father, Tom Weylin, arrives. Kevin—a white man—invents a cover story to explain their presence, asserting that Dana is a literate slave whose job is to help him with his writing. Rufus insists on having Dana by his side in the sickroom, which leads to tension with his unstable mother, Margaret.

Dana makes friends with the other slaves and Tom hires Kevin to teach his son. They settle into a routine, until Dana becomes uncomfortable with how easy it is. She realizes that slavery is a mental degradation, not just a physical one. When Tom discovers her teaching slave children to read, he knocks her to the ground and beats her. Before Kevin can reach her, she is returned to 1976.

The Fight

After eight days Dana is dragged back to a clearing where Rufus is fighting for his life. He has attempted to rape Alice Greenwood, and her husband Isaac is beating him to death. When Dana intervenes, Isaac and Alice flee the scene. She and Rufus return to the house—a large, wealthy Maryland plantation—and she learns that Kevin has been gone for two years, and Margaret has left. Dana nurses Rufus back to health, and he mails a letter to Kevin for her.

Alice and Isaac are caught, and his ears are cut off before he is sold. Rufus buys Alice and brings her home near death. Dana nurses her back to health. There is still no word from Kevin, and Dana sends more letters. Rufus gives Dana a horrible ultimatum—either she makes Alice consent to having sex with him, or he will have her beaten into submission. Alice, weary and terrified, agrees.

Discovering that Rufus never sent any of her letters to Kevin, Dana escapes, but is caught and whipped. Tom sends for Kevin, and he arrives as Dana reaches her breaking point. Riding away, Rufus shoots at them, and they are dragged back to the present.

The Storm

Back in 1976, Kevin finds it impossible to adjust. Dana finds herself pulled back again. Rufus is very ill. Dana helps him recover, but is unable to help Tom when he collapses with a heart attack. Blaming her, Rufus sends her into the fields, and then pulls her back out to help his mother, now a laudanum addict.

Alice and Rufus have a child, Joe. She teaches

Joe to read, and Rufus begins to love his son. Alice has a daughter, Hagar—Dana's ancestor. Dana agrees to help Alice escape as soon as Hagar is old enough. When Rufus sells a slave as a punishment for being too friendly with Dana she tries to stop him, but he punches her in the face. She slits her wrists and awakes in 1976.

The Rope

Fifteen days later, on the Fourth of July holiday, Dana is pulled back for the last time. She finds Rufus on the brink of suicide because Alice is dead. As a punishment for trying to run, Rufus moved their children to Baltimore, and told Alice that he'd sold them. Despairing, she took her own life.

After the funeral, tension mounts between Dana and Rufus, culminating in a confrontation in which he tries to rape her. She stabs him, and he dies clutching her. She is pulled back to the present with her arm crushed in the wall. Everything below her elbow—where Rufus grabbed her—is pulverized.

Epilogue

Dana recovers; she and Kevin discover that Weylin plantation was burnt to the ground the night Dana killed Rufus, and his death was attributed to the fire. The slaves were all sold. They realize that the murder was covered up, and accept that they will never know the rest.

Characters

Carrie

A mute slave, Carrie is a good friend to Dana. Most people believe that she is mentally impaired because of her handicap, but she is not. Carrie comforts Dana after Tom's death and explains that the slaves are better off under Rufus' ownership; if Rufus were dead, the slaves would be separated from their friends and families. She also comforts Dana when she is derided as being more white than black. Dana appreciates and values her friendship.

Jake Edwards

Jake Edwards is one of the overseers hired to manage the field hands. "It was amazing how much misery the man could cause doing the same job Luke had managed to do without hurting anybody," Dana observes. He forces Dana to do laundry by threatening her with a whipping.

Evan Fowler

Evan Fowler is the second overseer Dana encounters on the Weylin plantation. At first she believes that he is harmless, but his brutality proves that he is a cruel and unforgiving man.

Dana Franklin

An aspiring African-American writer, Dana Franklin is shocked when she is suddenly transported back into the past to save the life of her white ancestor, Rufus Weylin. Nothing in her life has prepared her for experiencing the South in the early nineteenth century. She witnesses the whipping of Alice Greenwood's father on her second visit, and the vivid sounds and smells make her realize that "I was probably less prepared for the reality [of violence] than the child crying not far from me."

As she later tells Kevin, "the more I think about it, the harder it is for me to believe I could survive even a few more trips to a place like that." She considers herself—a black woman—"the worst possible guardian" for Rufus, for "I would have all I could do to look after myself." She does not shrink from the task, however, because she knows her family's existence depends on her success. In addition, she thinks "I would … maybe plant a few ideas in [Rufus'] mind that would help both me and the people who would be his slaves in the years to come."

As her visits to the past become longer and more involved, Dana enjoys a privileged status in the Weylin household. She is disturbed by how easily she seems to acclimate to her new role, but realizes that this is because most of the time she can act as an observer. As time goes on, however, she is drawn more deeply into the pain of slavery.

When Rufus convinces Dana to persuade Alice to sleep with him in order to avoid a beating, she wonders if she has become "submissive"—the "white nigger" Alice accuses her of being. Yet as Carrie reassures her, the black "doesn't come off."

Dana eventually comes to understand that she is like the other slaves. All of them "have to do things they don't like to stay alive and whole." In the end, however, Dana realizes that although it would be "so easy" to submit to Rufus' advances, "A slave was still a slave. Anything could be done to her." She is unable to submit, and kills Rufus. Although she returns to the present, she loses an arm on the journey: her escape, like everything else about her experience, has exacted a high cost.

Edana Franklin

See Dana Franklin

Kevin Franklin

Kevin is Dana's husband. He is an "unusual-looking white man, his face young, almost unlined, but his hair completely gray and his eyes so pale as to be almost colorless." His pale eyes make him "seem distant and angry whether he was or not," but he has a winning grin that "completely destroyed the effect of his eyes."

When Dana meets him at the temp agency, she enjoys his sense of humor, and recognizes that this fellow writer "was like me—a kindred spirit crazy enough to keep on trying." After four months together Kevin proposes, and the two marry despite the objections of their families.

Kevin is a kind and thoughtful husband. After Dana's second trip into the past, although he has little understanding of what has happened to her, he prepares a survival kit and ties it to her waist while she is sleeping. When she begins to disappear a third time, he embraces her and is pulled back into the past as well. Although she knows she will be safer with him there, Dana fears what it will do to his mind: "I didn't want this place to touch him except through me."

There are signs that perhaps her fears are valid. Dana is upset by how easily they both seem to adjust to their new roles as slave and master, and how Kevin sometimes finds the idea of living in the past interesting. Kevin is not really suited to the past, as Sarah observes: "He'd get in trouble every now and then 'cause he couldn't tell the difference 'tween black and white." The five years he spends in the past scar him terribly.

When they finally return to the present, he seems colder, angrier, and more solitary. Nevertheless, while the long separations have not helped the couple's relationship, in some ways they have reinforced their sense of being kindred spirits. As Dana notes, "It was easy for us to be together, knowing we shared experiences no one else would believe."

Alice Greenwood

Dana has already figured out that Alice Greenwood is her ancestor when she meets the child on her second trip to the past. Rufus considers Alice his friend, and notes that she is a free black, "born free like her mother." Alice obviously knows the pains of slavery, however, for her father is a slave on the Weylin plantation who is brutally whipped when he is discovered visiting his wife without a pass.

Dana does not meet her ancestor again until her fourth visit, when Isaac almost kills Rufus. Although Alice is furious over Rufus' attempt to rape her, she persuades Isaac not to kill him, knowing it would mean Isaac's death if he were captured. Instead she tries to escape with him.

Alice and Isaac are captured, however, and the penalty for helping him to escape is a beating, after which she is sold into slavery. Rufus buys her, paying twice the market price. Dana nurses her back to health and tells Alice the truth about what happened when she cannot remember it.

Alice and Dana become close friends. The two women look alike, and Rufus considers them two halves of one woman. Alice's "erratic" relationship with Dana is sister-like: "sometimes needing my friendship, trusting me with her dangerous longings for freedom …; and sometimes hating me, blaming me for her trouble."

As the years pass, Alice becomes hard and

bitter. She loses two of her first three children to illness, and the other slaves shun her because of her relationship with Rufus. After the birth of Hagar, Alice resolves to escape. Alice commits suicide after Rufus moves her children away.

Alice Jackson

See Alice Greenwood

Isaac Jackson

Isaac Jackson is Alice's husband. When he discovers Rufus trying to rape his wife, he beats him, which brings Dana into the past for the fourth time. After the incident, he and Alice attempt to escape. They are captured, however, and Isaac is sold after being beaten and mutilated.

Sam James

Sam James is a big, muscular slave who attempts to get Dana to dance with him at Christmas. She warns him not to speak to her after Rufus threatens to sell any slave she might want to "jump the broom" with. After Rufus allows Dana to teach some of the young slave children to read, Sam James asks her to teach his brother and sister as well. When Sam is sold three days later, Dana's anger with Rufus leads her to attempt suicide and return to the present.

Liza

Liza is a slave who is sent into the fields after Alice has healed enough from her beating to take her job. Her resentment of Alice—and by extension Dana, who healed Alice—leads her to betray Dana. Alice, Tess, and Carrie perceive this as a betrayal of the slave community, and beat her severely as a warning. "Now she's more scared of us than of Mister Tom," Alice says.

Luke

Luke is Nigel's father. Dana meets Luke after Rufus breaks his leg. He is the "driver" of the plantation, a type of black overseer whose job it is to manage the field hands. She learns later that Tom grew tired of his attitude and sold him.

Aunt Mary

Aunt Mary's job is to look after the children; unfortunately, she is senile. Yet people are more likely to rely on her knowledge of herbal medicine than on the white doctor.

Nigel

Nigel is a slave and Rufus' playmate. As an adult, he becomes a house slave—one with a privileged position. He grows into a big, handsome man like his father, with the same desire for freedom. After an attempt to run away, he is severely whipped.

Nigel has enough influence with Rufus to stand up to the overseer Jake Edwards. After he marries Carrie and starts a family with her, the Weylins feel assured that Nigel will not make another attempt to run away. He still dreams of freedom, however. As he tells Dana, "It's good to have children…. But it's so hard to see them be slaves."

Sarah

Sarah is the plantation cook. She is kind and patient with Dana and is fond of Rufus. Nevertheless, she resents him for selling away most of her children. She does not trust whites, for she learned from her first master—the father of her first child—that even promises made in love are "just another lie."

Sarah is outspoken and opinionated. After Luke is sold, however, Sarah appears more cautious. "She had done the safe thing—accepted a life of slavery because she was afraid." Dana comes to appreciate the warnings and wisdom Sarah shares with her.

Tess

Tess is a young slave Dana meets on her fourth trip into the past. Dana helps Tess with her work because Tom injured her during a sexual experience. Tess loses her laundry job after Tom discards her, leaving her to the attentions of Jake Edwards. Edwards sends her to the fields so he can keep watch over her. Eventually she is sold. Her experiences exemplify the inhuman conditions slaves face. As Tess says, "You do everything they tell you ... and they still treat you like an old dog."

Doctor West

Doctor West is the Weylin family doctor. He is "pompous, condescending, and almost as ignorant medically as I was," as Dana describes him. His use of such methods as bleeding and purging, despite his good intentions, is harmful to his patients. Doctor West serves as another reminder to Dana that she is living in a very different age from her own.

Joe Weylin

Joe is the oldest surviving child of Alice Greenwood and Rufus Weylin. Initially a sickly child, he is also lively and bright. He is a good student and excels at his lessons. Rufus gradually comes to recognize his son, allowing him to call him "Daddy" after Alice's death.

Margaret Weylin

Margaret Weylin is the second wife of Tom Weylin. At first, she is ignorant and mean-spirited. Margaret hates Dana not only because she is an educated black but also because she is jealous that

Dana has both Kevin's and Rufus' favor. Dana comes to understand that a great part of Margaret's problem is boredom—she has nothing to occupy her time, and so spends it supervising and criticizing people in order to prove her worth.

After giving birth to stillborn twin boys, Margaret has a mental breakdown and is sent to stay with her sister in Baltimore. Rufus brings her back to the plantation after his father's death and asks Dana to care for her. While Margaret still insists on having things a certain way, she is calmer and introspective. Dana and Margaret eventually become friends.

Rufus Weylin

Dana finds Rufus a complex and contrary figure. He is an oddly appealing child, accepting of Dana and adventurous enough to help her escape on her second visit. Even as a boy, Rufus shows signs of a cold, possessive temper. When Margaret interrupts Dana, he berates her, just as his father Tom does: "His mouth was drawn into a thin straight line and his eyes were coldly hostile." As an adult, he tends to drink too much and will "pick a fight just out of meanness."

Rufus loves his childhood friend Alice, but it is a "destructive single-minded love" that is more about power than love. After she marries Isaac, Rufus attempts to rape her—an act that ironically leads to his purchase of Alice and the sale of her husband. He is "erratic, alternately generous and vicious," but Dana does not quite believe Sarah's warning that Rufus "says what will make you feel good—not what's true"; that is, until she discovers he has lied about sending her letters to Kevin. "I kept thinking I knew him, and he kept proving to me that I didn't."

Somehow Dana is able to forgive him for his possessiveness and cruelty. She recognizes that his behavior comes from pain, anger, or fear. His attempt to replace Alice with Dana, however, is the last straw for her. "I could accept him as my ancestor, my younger brother, my friend, but not as my master, and not as my lover."

Tom Weylin

Initially, Dana finds Tom Weylin a brutal and fearsome figure. He beats his son, Rufus; moreover, when his son breaks his leg his only concern seems to be what it will cost him. He shows no hesitation in whipping slaves and has no qualms about separating slave families.

Tom sometimes demonstrates a sense of fairness and gratitude. He allows Dana to choose whether to stay on the plantation or search for Kevin after her fourth arrival. He gives Dana a whipping after she makes an escape attempt, but "he didn't hurt you nearly as much as he's hurt others," Rufus tells her. After he discovers that Rufus broke his promise to let Kevin know of Dana's arrival, he sends word himself.

"Daddy's the only man I know," says Rufus,

"who cares as much about giving his word to a black as to a white." As Dana comes to understand, Tom Weylin "wasn't a monster at all. Just an ordinary man who sometimes did the monstrous things his society said were legal and proper."

Human Condition

As Dana soon discovers, the reality of slavery is even more disturbing than its portrayal in books, movies, and television programs. Before her journey into the past, Dana called the temp agency where she worked a "slave market," even though "the people who ran it couldn't have cared less whether or not you showed up to do the work they offered."

This turns out to be an ironic contrast to life at the Weylin plantation, where a slave who visits his wife without his master's permission is brutally whipped. Perhaps a more painful realization for Dana is how this cruel treatment oppresses the mind. "Slavery of any kind fostered strange relationships," she notes, for all the slaves feel the same strange combination of fear, contempt, and affection toward Rufus that she does.

At first she has difficulty comprehending Sarah's patience with a master who has sold off three of her children. Likewise, she observes that Isaac Greenwood "was like Sarah, holding himself back, not killing in spite of anger I could only imagine. A lifetime of conditioning could be overcome, but not easily."

"After being beaten following her attempt to

run away, however, Dana is tormented by doubts about her own resistance: "Why was I so frightened now—frightened sick at the thought that sooner or later, I would have to run again? ... I tried to get away from my thoughts, but they still came. *See how easily slaves are made?* they said."

In the end, however, Dana realizes that she cannot bring herself to accept slavery, even to a man who would not physically hurt her. "A slave was a slave. Anything could be done to her," Dana thinks as she sinks the knife into Rufus' side.

Choices and Consequences

The whole reason behind Dana's travels into the past is survival. Dana finds herself driven to save Rufus not just to ensure his existence but also that of her whole family. Despite her modern education, Dana doubts that she has the strength and endurance that her ancestors had: "To survive, my ancestors had to put up with more than I ever could," she tells Kevin.

On her second trip to the past, her squeamishness keeps her from defending herself from a patroller. The next time, however, she is ready to maim to escape: "I could do it now. I could do anything." Nevertheless, she finds it ironic that her job is to protect a white man: "I was the worst possible guardian for him—a black to watch over him in a society that considered blacks subhuman, a woman to watch over him in a society that considered women perennial children."

Despite her doubts, she manages to save Rufus on several different occasions, and learns more about survival in the process. As she listens to the field hands talking in the cookhouse and observes the other house slaves, she gains information: "Without knowing it, they prepared me to survive."

The drive for survival is very strong, and for slaves this means making many painful choices. "Mama said she'd rather be dead than be a slave," Alice recalls, but Dana disagrees: "Better to stay alive…. At least while there's a chance to get free." Because she thinks she will have a better chance of survival if she befriends the Weylins, she accepts the role of slave during her stay on the plantation. As long as this is her choice and she still has some semblance of control over her life, she finds she can endure more than she ever anticipated.

Accepting this role, however, means that Dana must make some very painful choices. For instance, she agrees to convince Alice to sleep with Rufus willingly because she does not want to see her suffer another beating. She is a quiet and compliant worker, even though this makes the other slaves look at her suspiciously. As she explains to Sam, the field hands "aren't the only ones who have to do things they don't like to stay alive and whole." It is only when Rufus tries to take away the final bit of control she has—control over her body—that Dana kills him.

Appearances and Reality

The strange nature of their time travels causes Dana and Kevin to examine how much their perceptions truly reflect reality. When Dana returns from her first visit, Kevin has difficulty accepting her explanation of where she has been. Yet he has no alternate explanation for her sudden disappearance. "I know what I saw, and what I did —my facts," Dana tells him. "They're no crazier than yours."

After Dana's second trip, however, Kevin admits, "I wouldn't dare act as though I didn't believe. After all, when you vanish from here, you must go someplace." That he finally gets proof when he accompanies Dana on one of these trips does not lessen his point: to communicate with others, sometimes you must accept their perceptions of reality—no matter how strange—as valid.

Topics for Further Study

- Write a short story in which you

travel to the future. Describe this world. What has changed? Does racism still exist in this society?

- Read an original slave narrative of the 1800s, such as Frederick Douglass's *Narrative of the Life of Frederick Douglass* (1845) or Harriet Ja-cobs's *Incidents in the Life of a Slave Girl* (1861). Use the details of slave life to write a mock diary entry describing a typical day in the life of a slave.

- As an interracial couple, Kevin and Dana Franklin face legal obstacles to their marriage in the nineteenth century and social opposition in the twentieth. Do some research into interracial marriages: trace the history of miscegenation laws (laws regulating interracial relationships) and look up statistics. Are interracial marriages on the increase? Are they more or less likely to end in divorce? Write an essay discussing your findings.

- The Missouri Compromise of 1820 established a precedent for how the United States would deal with the issue of slavery. Research the history of laws and Supreme Court decisions concerning slavery between 1820 and 1860. Create a timeline tracing these developments, and accompany it with a map illustrating the addition of new slave and free states during the same period.

While Dana and Kevin are living together in the past, they discover another aspect of the conection between appearances and reality: sometimes when you fake an appearance, it begins to feel like reality. At first, Dana is only "pretending" to play the part of a slave, one who sleeps with her master because she has no choice. Although she knows in her heart that she and Kevin are married equals, she nevertheless feels strange when she sneaks in his room: "I felt almost as though I really was doing something shameful, happily playing whore for my supposed owner."

Later she realizes that she cannot continue to be just a modern observer playing the "role" of slave. She becomes involved: she quietly teaches Nigel to read, befriends Carrie and Alice, and plans her escape after being beaten. In the end she cannot fully accept the reality of life as a slave, however, and leaves the past by killing Rufus.

Difference

As a modern woman living in the past, Dana is different in experience and perspective from everyone around her. She is bound to feel alienated because she is so out of place. Ironically, however, it may be a shared sense of alienation that attracts her to others. When she wonders why she is drawn into the past to save Rufus, for instance, she thinks that their blood relationship does not quite explain it: "What we had was something new, something that didn't even have a name. Some matching strangeness in us that may or may not have come from being related."

Her relationship with Kevin is based on a similar sense of shared difference. When they first meet, Dana thinks he "was as lonely and out of place as I was." As she gets to know him, she understands that this loneliness makes him "like me —a kindred spirit crazy enough to keep on trying." On the plantation, Dana's closest friends are people who are similarly alienated from the slave community: Carrie because of her muteness, and Alice because of her role as Rufus' mistress.

Returning home does not cure Dana and Kevin of feeling out of place; it takes them a while to readjust to the twentieth century. Again, however, this alienation brings them together: "It was easy for us to be together, knowing we shared experiences no one else would believe."

Narrator/Point of View

Kindred uses a first-person narrator, which means that Dana is telling her story from her own perspective. She relates her own thoughts, feelings, perceptions, and experiences. Other characters— such as Rufus, Alice, and Kevin—are known to the reader only through her perceptions of them.

An advantage of first-person narration is that the reader can really identify with Dana. In addition, much of the plot is comprised of Dana's attempts to understand the society and the people of the past. Her perspective is paramount; in fact, if the reader did not know her thoughts and feelings, it could be difficult to perceive this type of "action."

Another important advantage of a first-person narrator is that it makes the story resemble the historical slave narratives of the past. In creating her own version of the slave narrative, Dana is echoing and extending these historical stories.

Flashback

A flashback is a literary device used to relate events that occurred before the beginning of the story. After a brief prologue, the main action of the story begins with Dana's first journey back into the past. The first two chapters are used to reveal the basic plot of the novel: Dana is being called back in time to rescue her ancestor.

The third and fourth chapters, however, open with a flashback to Dana and Kevin's courtship. This helps flesh out Kevin's character, as well as Dana and Kevin's relationship. This added depth is essential for the reader to understand their devotion to each other. Butler could have presented this information chronologically by describing the courtship at the very beginning of the novel. By presenting it in flashbacks, Butler can focus the opening on Dana's adventure and is thus able to immediately draw the reader into the action of the book.

Foreshadowing

Foreshadowing is a literary device used to hint at future events before they actually happen. In *Kindred*, the prologue actually takes place after the main action of the story, and thus provides the reader with a glimpse of the result of Dana's travels. "I lost an arm on my last trip home," Dana recalls in the first sentence of the novel. Her conversation with Kevin also reveals that the truth of what has happened to her is unbelievable.

This prologue prepares reader for two things: first, that Dana is about to recount events that are strange and unexplainable; second, it alerts readers that Dana's experience will involve serious violence that will permanently scar her.

Denouement

Sometimes called falling action, the *denouement* refers to the resolution of a story's conflict. (*Denouement* is a French word which means "the unknotting.") The *denouement* follows the climax of the conflict and traditionally provides a resolution to the primary plot situation as well as an explanation of secondary plot complications. This outcome does not always have to consist of a physical action; it can also involve a character's recognition of his or her state of mind or moral condition.

The *denouement* of *Kindred* does not strictly fit this definition, however. There is a resolution, for Dana returns to the present after her fight with Rufus, ending the essential conflict of the novel. Yet many secondary questions are never resolved. How was Dana pulled into the past in the first place? Why and how did she lose an arm on her last trip? What happened to Rufus and Alice's children —were they sold or freed?

Dana's search for answers at the end of the novel yields nothing. Critic Robert Crossley has suggested that this open-ended *denouement* serves a specific purpose. "Leaving the novel's ending rough-edged and raw like Dana's wound," he wrote in the introduction to the novel, "Butler leaves the reader uneasy and disturbed by the intersection of story and history rather than comforted by a tale that 'makes sense.'"

Science Fiction

While Butler maintained that *Kindred* is not really science fiction—there is no scientific explanation for Dana's voyages to the past—the time travel story is a staple of the genre. The first novel by English writer H. G. Wells, long considered one of the fathers of science fiction (along with Frenchman Jules Verne), was *The Time Machine* (1895).

Wells also used the device of time travel to dramatize human inequalities. Journeying into the distant future, Wells' traveler encounters two races, the Eloi and the Morlocks. The relationship between the pleasure-loving Eloi and the subterranean Morlocks serves as an ironic comment on the conflict between ruling and working classes of the late-nineteenth century's newly industrialized society.

In *Kindred* it is never explained *how* Dana is transported into the past, or why her arm should be severed upon her final return. While the novel contains elements of science fiction, it also works from the tradition of the slave narrative and the historical novel. As Crossley concluded, "Butler's novel is an experiment that resists easy classification by blurring the usual boundaries of genre."

The Missouri Compromise

The Missouri Compromise marked the first serious debate over the status of slavery in the growing United States, and provides an interesting look at how slavery was perceived at the time. In 1819 the territory of Missouri applied for admission to the Union. During the review process, Representative James Tallmadge of New York added an amendment that would outlaw slavery in Missouri. The House and Senate were divided over the amendment.

Eventually a compromise was reached: Missouri would be admitted as a slave state; Maine would be admitted as a free state; and slavery would be prohibited in the remaining portions of the Louisiana territory north of latitude 36 degrees 30 minutes north.

The debate over slavery was an important turning point in American history. Not because Northerners wanted to eliminate slavery—they were more concerned with limiting it than with eradicating it. Instead, it was the Southern attitude that showed a marked change from previous debates on the issue. In previous years, Southerners were defensive about the institution, and seemed only to tolerate it as a necessary evil.

However, during the debate over the Missouri Compromise, Southerners began to justify and even glorify slavery as a moral system. Attacks on it were considered attacks on the South itself. Attempts to limit slavery were similarly considered attacks on the sovereignty of Southern states.

The Missouri Compromise eased the tensions created by the slavery issue for several years, and set a precedent for further political settlements. Yet it wasn't long before the United States entered into a bloody Civil War.

Rebels and Abolitionists

Several highly publicized slave rebellions in the early nineteenth century reinforced the resolve of Southern slave owners to protect the institution of slavery. While there had been a few slave revolts in the 1700s, the largest occurred in the years just before the events of *Kindred*. In 1800, a revolt by more than one thousand slaves in Virginia was delayed by rainstorms; the leaders were captured before the revolt could be continued.

The largest U. S. slave rebellion occurred in 1811 in Louisiana, when some three to five hundred slaves marched from plantation to plantation gathering recruits and weapons. The rebellion ended when the slaves, led by freeman Charles Deslondes, encountered militia and U.S. military troops.

Another rebellion, which is mentioned in *Kindred* as one that frightened many slave owners, was the 1822 insurrection planned by Denmark

Vesey. A former slave who bought his freedom with lottery winnings, Vesey and nine thousand recruits planned to invade Charleston, South Carolina. Vesey's plans were betrayed, however, and he was captured and hanged before his plans could be carried out.

In *Kindred*, Kevin Franklin mentions that he was suspected of helping slaves to escape. Both whites and free blacks were involved in the Underground Railroad in the 1810s and 1820s, helping slaves to escape north. Nevertheless, the abolitionist movement—the drive to eliminate slavery completely—did not really get off the ground until the 1830s.

Most historians date the beginning of abolitionism to 1831, when William Lloyd Garrison began publishing his journal *The Liberator*. Before this time, most opponents of slavery proposed moderate solutions, such as compensating slave owners for emancipation or the emigration of free blacks to Africa. Garrison's journal, however, advocated immediate eradication of slavery everywhere in the United States. The American Anti-Slavery Society was founded in 1833, and was an important voice in the debates over slavery that led up to the Civil War.

Black Power and Black Pride

The "Black Power" movement of the late 1960s and 1970s grew out of the movement for civil rights. As efforts to integrate America were slow to progress, some African Americans came to believe that working within the white-dominated system was not an effective way to achieve their goals. Black Power advocates believed that blacks should celebrate their own heritage and culture. They should not depend on whites to help change the system, but should instead rely on their own communities for political and economic success.

Sometimes the rhetoric of the Black Power Movement was angry and polemic. For instance, many advocates believed that no whites were to be trusted. African Americans—often of older generations—who supported working within the system were often accused of being collaborators. It was this atmosphere of mistrust between different activist camps that was one of Butler's inspirations in writing *Kindred*.

There were groups within the Black Power movement, however, that were less radical and more willing to work within the system to affect political and social change. Their promotion of "Black Pride" led to an increased visibility of African American heritage and culture. In the 1970s African Americans had a growing influence on television, movies, and literature.

The most notable of these successes was the 1977 television miniseries *Roots*. Based on the novel by Alex Haley, this eight-part saga of one African American family captivated nearly 130 million viewers and spawned a new interest in genealogy (the study of family history). Thousands of Americans were inspired to research their own family backgrounds—just as Dana Franklin had to do to survive in Butler's novel.

Critical Overview

Although Butler's *Kindred* was only her fourth novel, published a mere three years after her 1976 debut, it did not take long for critics to praise its unusual qualities. In an early review of the novel, Joanna Russ asserted in the *Magazine of Fantasy and Science Fiction* that "*Kindred* is more polished than [Butler's] earlier work but still has the author's stubborn, idiosyncratic gift for realism." In particular, Russ hailed how the author "makes new and eloquent use" of the time-travel idea, and pointed out her skilled characterizations and fast-paced style.

While *Fantasy Review* contributor John R. Pfeiffer deemed *Kindred* a novel "of such special excellence that critical appreciation of [it] will take several years to assemble," such in-depth analyses soon followed.

In 1982 Beverly Friend examined how the time-travel plot of the novel served to highlight important feminist issues. "No one would intellectually argue against the proposition that life is better today for both men and women," the critic wrote in *Extrapolation*, "but few realize what ... [this novel has] didactically presented: that contemporary woman is not educated to survive, that she is as helpless, perhaps even more helpless, than her predecessors."

Subsequent analyses of *Kindred* have explored

how Dana's experiences as a twentieth-century writer and nineteenth-century slave have illuminated issues of sex, race, and history. Margaret Anne O'Connor, for instance, observed that it is not just the stark contrasts between Dana's two lives that are educational, but also the parallels: "Slowly [Dana and Kevin] also come to see the situations of virtual slavery in their own technological, twentieth-century culture," the author wrote in the *Dictionary of Literary Biography*. "Drawing an analogy between power relationships of the early nineteenth century and the home, office, and bedroom of contemporary America, *Kindred* offers readers a chance to evaluate the racial and sexual dimensions of both cultures."

Dana's experiences also allow her insight into the power that has allowed black women—supposedly powerless in a sexist and racist society—to persevere. According to Thelma J. Shinn, Dana learns to survive the travails of slavery by learning from black female mentors such as Sarah, an archetypal figure Shinn called "the wise witch." As the critic stated in *Conjuring: Black Women, Fiction, and Literary Tradition, "Kindred* shows that Butler's wise witches, her compassionate teachers armed with knives and cast-iron skillets, have survived and will survive, whether or not they are accepted by their society."

Not only does *Kindred* emphasize the power of those who are oppressed, it also reclaims history from the dominant culture, according to Adam McKible. In a 1994 *African American Review* article, the critic argued that *Kindred*, like other tales of African American women enduring slavery, forces the reader to reassess historical "truth" just by making a black woman the heroine. As a result, "the perspective of the black female slave, who finds herself at the bottom of the hierarchies of race, class, and gender ... can in fact become a powerful site of rebellion and self-assertion."

In addition, McKible underscored the way in which names can similarly become symbols of resistance. In *Kindred*, not only does Alice name her children after biblical survivors of slavery, but the protagonist asserts control by choosing to call herself Dana rather than Edana. Thus names "are crystallizations—constant reminders—of resistance and the will to freedom," according to McKible.

The analysis that *Kindred* attracts, even twenty years after its publication, seems to justify Robert Crossley's belief that "if any contemporary writer is likely to redraw science fiction's cultural boundaries and to attract new black readers—and perhaps writers—to this most distinctive of twentieth-century genres, it is Octavia Butler. More consistently than any other black author, she has deployed the genre's conventions to tell stories with a political and sociological edge to them, stories that speak to issues, feelings, and historical truths arising out of Afro-American experience."

Sources

Robert Crossley, in an introduction to *Kindred*, by Octavia Butler, Beacon Press, 1988, pp. ix-xxvii.

Beverly Friend, "Time Travel as a Feminist Didactic in Works by Phyllis Eisenstein, Marlys Millhiser, and Octavia Butler," in *Extrapolation*, Vol. 23, No. 1, Spring, 1982, pp. 50-5.

Adam McKible, "'These Are the Facts of the Darky's History': Thinking History and Reading Names in Four African American Texts," in *African American Review*, Vol. 28, No. 2, 1994, pp. 223-35.

Margaret Anne O'Connor, "Octavia E. Butler," in *Dictionary of Literary Biography*, Vol. 33: *Afro-American Fiction Writers After 1955*, edited by Thadious M. Davis and Trudier Harris, Gale Research Company, 1984, pp. 36-40.

John R. Pfeiffer, "Latest Butler a Delicious Confection," in *Fantasy Review*, Vol. 7, No. 6, July, 1984, p. 44.

Joanna Russ, in *Magazine of Fantasy and Science Fiction*, Vol. 58, No. 2, February, 1980, pp. 96-7.

Thelma J. Shinn, "The Wise Witches: Black Women Mentors in the Fiction of Octavia E. Butler," in *Conjuring: Black Women, Fiction, and Literary Tradition*, edited by Marjorie Pryse and Hortense J. Spillers, Indiana University Press, 1985, pp. 203-15.

For Further Study

Frances M. Beal, "Black Women and the Science Fiction Genre: Interview with Octavia M. Butler," in *Black Scholar*, Vol. 17, March-April, 1986, p. 14.

> An interview with Butler in which she discusses her childhood and other influences.

Teri Ann Doerksen, "Octavia E. Butler: Parables of Race and Difference," in *Into Darkness Peering: Race and Color in the Fantastic*, edited by Elisabeth Anne Leonard, Greenwood Press, 1997, pp. 21-34.

> Views Butler's novels as works that "have the potential to lead the once typical white or male reader into some (perhaps uncomfortable) realizations about his or her own society."

Sandra Y. Govan, "Homage to Tradition: Octavia Butler Renovates the Historical Novel," in *MELUS*, Vol. 13, Nos. 1-2, 1986, pp. 79-96.

> Provides a stylistic examination of Butler's novel, praising innovative aspects of her work.

Patricia Maida, "*Kindred* and *Dessa Rose:* Two Novels That Reinvent Slavery," in *CEA Magazine*, Vol. 4, No. 1, 1991, pp. 43-52.

> Traces the portrayal of slavery in
> both novels.

Veronica Mixon, "Futurist Woman: Octavia
Butler," in *Essence*, Vol. 15, April, 1979, pp. 12-13.

> A biographical article on Butler
> containing an interview with the
> author.

Burton Raffel, "Genre to the Rear, Race and Gender
to the Fore: The Novels of Octavia E. Butler," in
Literary Review, Vol. 38, Spring, 1995, pp. 453-61.

> Provides a thematic overview of
> Butler's novels, in particular the
> treatment of race and gender issues.

Hoda M. Zaki, "Utopia, Dystopia and Ideology in
the Science Fiction of Octavia Butler," in *Science
Fiction Studies*, Vol. 17, No. 2, 1990, pp. 239-51.

> Surveys the major themes of Butler's
> science fiction.

CPSIA information can be obtained
at www.ICGtesting.com
Printed in the USA
LVHW052317060219
606704LV00008B/77/P